How to Survive an Italian Family

How to Survive an Italian Family

Rick Detorie

A PERIGEE BOOK

Perigee Books
are published by
The Putnam Publishing Group
200 Madison Avenue
New York, NY 10016

Design by Anne Scatto/Levavi & Levavi

Typeset by Fisher Composition, Inc.

Library of Congress Cataloging-in-Publication Data

Detorie, Rick.
How to survive an Italian family.

1. Italian American families—Anecdotes,
facetiae, satire, etc.   I. Title.
PN6231.I85D48   1987   306.8′5′08951073   87-2447
ISBN 0-399-51359-0

Printed in the United States of America
1   2   3   4   5   6   7   8   9   10

Special thanks to the members of my immediate family. I couldn't have done it without all 9,768 of you.

This book is dedicated with love to Elizabeth Epifanio and Gino Speca, both of whom were an inspiration to me during the writing of this book and will continue to inspire me forever.

DISCLAIMER

This is a work of fiction. This is also a piece of work, let me tell you. None of the characters or events depicted in this book is intended to represent individuals, living or dead, nor is any intended to be representative of all Italians. The experiences related in this book are based on my own personal experiences and embellished by my over-active imagination. It's a loving, though exaggerated, look at my life in an Italian family, a humorous poke at my loved ones and myself. It is this ability to laugh at ourselves that has helped us, over the years, get through the hard times and, at the same time, made the good times that much more enjoyable.

Rick Detorie

CONTENTS

INTRODUCTION

Whether you're born into an Italian family or marry into it, being a member is seldom an easy assignment. It's a tough job, one that requires diligence, perseverance, a thick skin, unusual communication skills, and a hearty appetite. The Italian family teems with love, drama, aggravation, guilt, and passion; and any person who's unprepared to handle massive doses of any or all of these elements is fated to wind up under the cellar steps, a drooling heap of mangled neuroses.

This does not mean that all Italian families are this intense, nor, for that matter, are all Italian families exactly alike. There are some differences. One family, for example, may contain more aggravation and less drama; and another may lean toward more passion and less guilt, or more love and less drama, and so on. The mixtures are rich and varied, and each family prides itself on its uniqueness. However, there is one element that's common to all Italian families, and that element is surprise. Hang around an Italian family for a little while and you're bound to run into a few surprises. Hang around for a longer length of time and, if you're one of the uninitiated, you'll be not only surprised but shocked, charmed, intrigued, everything but bored.

The purpose of this book is to bring to light some of the traits that are common to many Italian families and, in doing so, to expose some of the surprises that lie within. Once you know what to expect, perhaps you'll be better prepared to cope with your own family situation. Knowledge is the key to preparedness, and preparedness is the key to survival.

So, read the book; learn all you can; then take the Italian Family SurvivalTest at the end of the book. With luck, and armed with the knowledge to be acquired here, you just might be able to survive an Italian Family.

MAMMA MIA!

The Italian mother comes in many shapes and sizes. The stereotypical Mama Italiana is a scrupulous housekeeper, a dynamic cook, a prolific baby-maker, and an endless worrier when it comes to her children; but any stereotype is just that, a stereotype, and stereotypes don't always make the transition to real life.

Probably the only characteristic that one can safely say is common to all Italian mothers is their undying devotion to their children. They *love* their kids. To the Italian mom, those bambini are the most perfect little angels this side of the pearly gates. No matter how rotten her kids may be; no matter how much trouble they get into, the Italian mom steadfastly stands by her own. No one but she has the right to criticize her offspring, and she's not about to, at least not publicly.

Do you think Signora Mussolini ever uttered a bad word about her son, Benito? Of course not. She recognized his good points. He got the trains to run on time, didn't he? The critics always tend to overlook little Benito's many fine accomplishments, but they're quick to pounce on him (and rip out his mother's heart in the process) over one or two minor blunders, like World War II.

If an Italian child, God forbid, does get himself into trouble, then to his mom, there must be a good reason. For example, if little Frankie gets caught breaking windows down at the foam rubber factory, it's because:

A. He's been hanging around with that Calucci boy, a bad apple if ever there was one.
B. He ate too much junk food at the ball game and didn't know what he was doing.
C. He takes after his father's side of the family.

Sure, Frankie was caught red-handed, but it wasn't his fault, so he's not really guilty. Deep in her heart Mom knows that Frankie's a good kid. He's just misunderstood.

Oftentimes even the most persuasive evidence is not enough to convince an Italian mom of her child's guilt.

Take the case of Danny P. When told that 50,000 people saw Danny trip a cop at a rock concert, his mother replied, "A rock concert?! What do they know? They're all on drugs at those things! My Danny's innocent! He didn't do it. And if he did do it, he didn't mean to—so it's not his fault."

Her energetic defense of her children does not mean that the Italian mother is a pushover in the discipline department. Not in the least. Remember that she's unwilling to criticize her errant children *publicly*. Behind closed doors, it's a different story. Punishment from an Italian mother is swift and exact. It comes in several forms:

A. A quick rap to the back of the head.
B. Threats
   1. "Don't think I'm going to forget about this too soon!"
   2. "I can't stand to think about what your father's going to do when he finds out—and he *will* find out!"
   3. "Keep this up and you'll end up like Louie Balducci, a man who cleans other people's fish for a living."
C. Guilt
   1. "What did I do to deserve this?"
   2. "Haven't I suffered enough already?"
   3. "Here, take the car keys and drive me directly to:
      a. the poorhouse."
      b. the nut house."
      c. my grave."
D. All of the above

If worrying were an Olympic event, Italian mothers would sweep the medals every time. Italian mothers are among the greatest worriers in the world. They worry about big things like war, famine, pestilence,

14

Mother's guilt.

and irregularity; and they worry about little things like daytime soaps, crooked lotteries, and that odd-looking fungus growing on the dog's face.

Unlike Italian fathers who, though fraught with worry, never show it,* Italian moms shamelessly display their anxieties. They wear their worries as they would wear a big fur coat, and flounce about the house. They frown. They pace. They wring their hands. They talk to the ceiling, saying things like: "Why don't they ever listen to me?"; "Why hasn't she called?"; and every mother's favorite: "Where are we going to get that kind of money?"

---

*It takes an average of thirty-seven years for an Italian father (usually on his deathbed) to admit that yes, he was worried sick about little Patricia that time she had a nosebleed when she was four.

15

In church, Italian mothers light candles to St. Monica (the patron saint of mothers), St. Nicholas of Myra (children), St. Joseph (husbands), St. Thomas Aquinas (students), St. Martin de Porres (hairdressers), and if she's wealthy and has servant problems, St. Adelard (gardeners).

Italian mothers sit on the edge of their children's beds and study their little faces with pained expressions. They worry about the past: "Maybe that extra pinch of garlic was too much." They worry about the present: "Oh, please don't let Gino cut loose with a swearword during Father Sircosa's visit." They worry about the future: "Who's going to make homemade Play-doh for these kids if I drop dead tomorrow?"

A recent survey shows that Italian mothers spend ninety-six percent of their waking hours worrying about their children. (Their sleeping hours are ninety-eight percent.) The following list, taken from the same survey, covers the ten greatest fears that Italian mothers suffer every morning on behalf of their school-age children.

THE ITALIAN MOTHER'S EARLY MORNING WORRY LIST

1. What if I go to wake her up and she's been kidnapped by gypsies?
2. What if he catches pneumonia from not wearing his slippers to breakfast?
3. What if she chokes to death on a Fruit Loop?
4. What if the school-bus driver is a lush and crashes into a prison farm?
5. What if the school is attacked by Protestant terrorists?
6. What if he bleeds to death from a paper cut because the school nurse isn't a mother and doesn't understand these things?
7. What if she goes blind from sitting in the back row?
8. What if the little scab on his chin doesn't heal before the school pictures are taken?
9. What if Johnny Cristono steals her lunch and she starves to death?
10. What if he eats cafeteria food and dies from cholesterol before he's fifty?

Sometimes an Italian mother's worrying suffers from overexposure. Too much pacing, posturing, and pleading, and the children begin to

More of Mother's guilt.

suffer from AB: Anxiety Burnout. They're no longer able to hear their mothers' rantings and in some cases they begin to sleep well at night.

When this kind of apathy sets in, Italian mothers switch to automatic pilot. They continue to worry, but they try to hide it. This method is just as effective as the loud torments of the worried-sick mother. A strategically placed sigh or a look of quiet desperation can be like a giant vacuum cleaner, sucking a child's attention like a sack of cheap lint.

To see an example of this silent method of suffering, witness the following scene between an Italian mother and her two teenage daughters as the daughters depart for an outing at a lake.

The mother heaves a mournful sigh and sadly kisses each daughter on her forehead as they head out the door.

"Oh, *please,* Mother. Don't be so dramatic. We'll be real careful."

"That's right. We'll wear our seat belts and I'll drive very carefully."

The mother sorrowfully shakes her head as she smooths her younger daughter's collar.

"Honestly, Mother, sometimes you're such a martyr! We'll wear our life jackets!"

"We won't swim for three hours after we eat!"

"We won't go in the deep water!"

"We won't talk to any boys!"

The mother smiles weakly, certain in the knowledge that she'll never see her two daughters again.

"All right, you win! We won't go."

"Are you satisfied now?"

"No, no," says the mother. "I want you both to go and have a good time. Don't even think about me back here, all alone. I'll be all right. Really. Go! Go! Enjoy yourselves."

The daughters went to the lake. They had a fairly decent time, but not a great time, because they knew that their poor little mother was sitting at home, worried sick about them.

What follows is another example of an Italian mother trying to camouflage her anxieties in the guise of a cheery letter written to her daughter at college.

Dear Annie,
How are you doing?
Everyone here is fine.
Uncle Mike is doing much better.
Last Sunday we attended your cousin Gracie's graduation. It was real nice. Lots of her girlfriends from the old school were there.
After the ceremony Aunt Rena had a party at her house and served cake and her meatball surprise.
The weather has been real nice. It's been in the mid-80s.
I've been busy crocheting your brother a nice afghan, though the colors would look better in your room.
Take it easy and don't work so hard.

Love, Mom.

Now, with a look at what's written between the lines, the experienced Italian child sees a different story:

Dear Annie,
How are you doing?
And how would I know? You never call or write.

19

Everyone here is fine.

If you don't count me, that is.

Uncle Mike is doing much better.

Yeah, but after being laid up in the hospital for six weeks, you should see the medical bills. If insurance doesn't cover it he'll probably have to sell that house and he and your Aunt Dehlia will have to move in with us; and, my God, I dread the thought of it!

Last Sunday we attended your Cousin Gracie's graduation. It was real nice. Lots of her girlfriends from the old school were there.

Yeah, lots of girlfriends. I swear, if that girl doesn't drop some of that weight, we'll never see her with any boyfriends; and then she'll end up living at home for the rest of her life with Aunt Rena and Uncle Jimmy, like that Roselli boy who lives with his parents and does nothing all day but talk to the TV in his shorts.

After the ceremony Aunt Rena had a party at her house and served cake and her meatball surprise.

It was a surprise, all right. It was a surprise that anybody could keep it down. I was afraid your poor grandmother was going to keel over from meatball poisoning.

The weather has been real nice. It's been in the mid-80s.

It's the humidity that's killing us.

I've been crocheting your brother a nice afghan,

Not that he'll ever appreciate it

though the colors would look better in your room.

I only hope and pray that you survive college in one piece and make it back to see your old room again.

Take it easy and don't work so hard.

Remember what happened to Vera's cousin, Felice, who worked too hard, had a nervous breakdown, and now invites livestock in for coffee.

Love, Mom.

Or have you forgotten?

SURVIVAL TIP # 1

Never break your mother's heart. This means that you should never kill one of your siblings, hang out with tattooed people, or forget your lunch. This also means that you should always eat everything on your plate, have pleasant friends with good manners, and remember your galoshes.

SURVIVAL TIP #2

When asking an Italian mother for advice, listen attentively to everything she has to say on the subject, then go out and do what you had intended in the first place.

"THIS IS GOING TO KILL YOUR FATHER."

It's easy to spot the Italian dad. Immediately following a large meal, he's the gentleman snoring away on the Barcalounger, a placid island oblivious to the sea of family noise and turmoil churning in the room around him. The Italian father is also one of those fellows standing against the back wall of the church during Mass who swings into action with the collection plate and slips outside during Communion to sneak a cigarette. He's also the generous guy with the ready cash, his children's guaranteed first sale when they're out hawking candy bars, magazine subscriptions, and raffle tickets for the school pledge drives. Good old Dad.

Although it's easy enough to recognize the Italian father, it's much more difficult getting to *know* the man. This is because so many Italian fathers fancy themselves as the strong, silent type. They don't talk much. They're content to sit calmly by and allow the wife and children to freely express themselves until somebody gets out of line and Dad is called into action.

Because Dad speaks less often than anyone else in the family, when he *does* say something, it carries more weight, taking on the gravity of a pronouncement or a decree. When Mother tells Junior to wash his face and hands, the kid splashes a little water on himself, messes up her towels a bit, and he's done. But when that same child's father clears his throat, looks directly into his son's face and tells him to wash up, the kid scrubs as if his life depended on it, because he knows that if Dad has to show Junior how to wash, there will be a couple of layers of skin left back in the washbasin.

Some Italian children think that because Dad is nonvocal that he's uncommunicative. These children are either inexperienced or just not paying attention. For, experienced Italian children can interpret their fathers' pauses, body and facial expressions, and their occasional non sequiturs, and use these means of communication to experience rich and rewarding relationships with their dads.

The following, an actual conversation between an Italian father and his adult daughter during a visit he has made to her apartment across town, while appearing at first glance to be superficial, with few feelings expressed and little information imparted by the father, is upon closer examination a serious heart-to-heart on the part of the father.

"Daddy, I'm so glad you stopped by! How are you?"

"Traffic was hell."

She pulls two mugs from a shelf above the stove.

"How about some coffee, Pop? It's a fresh pot."

"You know, Tina, your Uncle Dino hasn't left his house for months. Your mother's worried about him. He sits in there all day watching TV with the shades pulled down."

"Oh . . . uh, that's a shame. Do you want to talk about it?"

"Nah. There's nothing to talk about."

There's a long pause as father and daughter sit in silence at the kitchen table, sipping coffee.

"So, Pop, what's going on back at the house?"

"Ah, same old thing. Your mother, your grandmother, your sister Ellie. You know."

They sit for a while longer, then Tina points toward the window.

"Tell me. What do you think of my kitchen curtains? I made them myself, if you can believe that."

"Do you need some money, Tina?" He reaches into his back pocket for his wallet.

"No, Daddy, really. I don't need anything right now. I'm just glad to see you."

"Here. You never know when you might need a little extra. Take it."

He presses a few bills into her hand. They stand up. She kisses him on the cheek.

"Thanks, Pop."

"I gotta go. You take care now, hear? You know how your mother worries."

"Good-bye, Pop."

"Good-bye."

He walks out the door and disappears down the staircase.

On the surface of this conversation there doesn't seem to be much real communication going on. But, as the following translation of the father's conversation makes clear, a lot more was felt and said by the father and understood by the daughter than is evident to the casual observer.

"Daddy, I'm so glad you stopped by! How are you?"

"Traffic was hell."

"But hey, you're my beautiful darling daughter and I would have climbed over Vesuvius in a truss in order to see you, if only for just a little while."

"How about some coffee, Pop? It's a fresh pot."

"You know, Tina, your Uncle Dino hasn't left his house for months. Your mother's worried about him. He sits in there all day watching TV with the shades pulled down."

"Your mother's not the only one worried about him. I'm worried about him. He's nuts! Can you imagine being so depressed you don't want to see your family, your friends, your own kids!? I hope to God I'm never feeling that bad."

"Oh . . . uh, that's a shame. Do you want to talk about it?"

"Nah. There's nothing to talk about."

"So, Pop, what's going on back at the house?"

"Ah, same old thing. Your mother, your grandmother, your sister Ellie. You know."

"If you only did know! Give me about six weeks and I might have enough time to fill you in! I could tell you about your grandmother, who every morning walks up Grandview Hill to visit her friend Pasqualina, then every afternoon calls me to come get her because she can't figure out how to get back down the hill; or I could tell you about my cousin, Fat Joe, who plans to bring his whole family to stay with us for a month again this summer, but I haven't had the nerve to tell your mother because the last time they visited they broke every chair in the house and ate us out of house and home; or I could tell you about your sister Ellie. Dio! Fifteen years old, and she dresses like a dance hall floozy! They all do, those kids her age. I think that in the mornings, after she leaves the house, she puts on makeup and then removes it before she comes home. From the looks of her friends,

24

they're putting it on with a spatula! Believe me, my life's not exactly one big picture postcard."

"Tell me. What do you think of my kitchen curtains? I made them myself, if you can believe that."

"Do you need some money, Tina?"

"I love you dearly and I want to show you that I love you, and this is the best way I know how. I was never one to display much physical attention, especially after you girls grew up and began to develop, well, you know, began to develop; and I have a difficult time saying the words, 'I love you,' so please accept the money."

"Thanks, Pop."

"I gotta go. You take care now, hear? You know how your mother worries."

"You know how I worry."

"Good-bye, Pop."

"Good-bye."

"I love you."

Silent communication is not the only method used by Italian fathers to converse with their children. Other methods of communication used by Italian dads are:

1. The Quick Rap to the Back of the Head.
2. The Fist Pounded on the Dinner Table.
3. Power of Attorney.

The first two methods are self-explanatory. The third method, Power of Attorney, is one in which the father actually takes it upon himself to speak for his wife, the child's mother. As Mother's "attorney," or mouthpiece, the father uses such popular phrases as: "Your mother wants to know," "You're breaking your mother's heart," and the perennial favorite, "This is going to kill your mother."

By acting as Mother's mouthpiece, the father is able to mask his true feelings by pretending to be the messenger who merely reports the concerns and fears of the child's mother. By focusing on the mother as the primary source of anxiety and love, the father is able to deflect attention from himself, becoming an innocent bystander in the process, thus shedding himself of the "unmanly" trait of expressing direct concern for his children.

One of the side effects of the Power of Attorney Method of Father-Child Communication is guilt. As Mother's spokesman, Father is able

The last thing in the world that Italian fathers want to discuss with their children is sex education. However, an Italian dad sometimes forces himself to have an in-depth (for him) discussion with one of his kids on the subjects of sex, love, and morality.

to use Mother's feelings to trigger guilt in his offspring. For example, when a father tells the son who has just bought a motorcycle that it will break his mother's heart, it conjures in that child's mind visions of his mother lying awake in bed, waiting for the late-night phone call from the state police, of his mom collapsing into a sobbing heap in the hospital emergency room, and of his little mother being helped to her feet at the edge of her son's open grave. Guilt can sometimes be a very effective weapon in an Italian family, regardless of who uses it.

What follows is a long-distance telephone conversation between an Italian son and his father. Note the father's expert use of Power of Attorney:

"Hello?"

"Hey, Micky, is that you? What time is it there? What's the weather like? I hear noises. Who's there with you?"

"Oh, hi, Dad. No one's here. I'm washing dishes. You hear me washing dishes."

"Washing dishes? Your mother and I thought you had a nice apartment with an automatic dishwasher. What's the matter, it's broken?"

"It's not broken, Dad. I'm washing these dishes by hand because I don't have a full load for the dishwasher."

"He doesn't have a full load for the dishwasher, Isabelle. What do you mean you don't have a full load?"

"It's just the lunch dishes, that's all, Dad."

"Lunch dishes? Your mother wants to know what's the matter. Aren't you eating three squares a day?"

"Sure. I had dinner out tonight."

"O Dio, restaurant food every night! If your mother hears about this it will kill her. Isabelle, come over here and listen to this! Your oldest son eats greasy restaurant food every night! What? Who knows where! Burger joints, saloons . . ."

"Hello, Mom?"

"She can't come to the phone, Micky. She went upstairs to get aspirin. I only hope she makes it, what with her bad heart an all. If she thinks you're not eating right, it could send her right over the edge. No lie. It's been one thing after another. First that thing with your Uncle Dominick and the fish, and now this. Promise me you're taking good care of yourself, for your mother's sake."

"Yeah, yeah, I'm doing all right, Dad. Plenty of sleep, good food, I'm taking good care of myself. I'm real healthy, honest."

"If you say so, Micky, I believe you. I'm just thinking of your mother, is all."

"I understand, Dad. Thanks for worrying about me, uh . . . I mean thank Mom for worrying about me. I've gotta go now. I'll talk to you later."

"Okay, so long, Micky."

It should be fairly obvious from this conversation that the father was using Micky's mother as a means of expressing his own feelings about his son. It's more than fairly obvious when one learns that the mother wasn't with Micky's father at the time of the conversation. She was in Trenton, visiting her cousin Barbara.

SURVIVAL TIP #3

Never ask an Italian father any question that requires more than a grunt as an answer.

SURVIVAL TIP #4

How to survive an Italian father: Never break your mother's heart.

... AND BAMBINO
<u>MAKES TEN.</u>

Italians have children for the same reasons most people have children: to carry on the family name, pressure from parents who want to become grandparents, and because someone didn't want to make a trip to the drugstore.

Italian children aren't much different from other children, there just seem to be more of them. Italian kids are as moody, high-strung, intelligent, angelic, dirty, mischievous, annoying, snotty, cocky, and noisy as other children. The only obvious physical difference is that Italian kids seem to be better fed than most other kids.

Although many modern Italian families try to deny it, the traditional Italian family was, and in most cases still is, a sexist family. Italian fathers want sons; sons to carry on the family name; sons to continue the family business; sons to get somebody else's daughters into trouble about the time puberty kicks in.

The oldest son has the choicest spot in the Italian family. As the firstborn male, he automatically acquires preferential treatment and higher expectations from the adults; and from his younger siblings he receives resentment, jealousy, and the occasional death threat.

None of the boys, including the younger ones are expected to do traditional "woman's work" around the house, like dusting, washing dishes, or making the beds. Instead, they're required to do typical

WHY ITALIAN WOMEN DON'T DO YARD WORK

EARLY ONE SUMMER MORNING, LINDA REPORTS FOR YARD WORK AT HER GRANDFATHER'S HOUSE...

...WHERE SHE MOWS...

...TRIMS...

...RAKES...

...AND CLEANS.

AT 3:30 P.M. COUSIN NICKY JOINS HER AND SWEEPS THE SIDEWALK.

HI, NICKY.

HI, LINDA.

AT 4:00 P.M. GRAMPS RETURNS HOME FROM THE ITALIAN DELI.

HI, GRANDPOP! I MOWED, TRIMMED, RAKED, AND CLEANED...

...AND COUSIN NICKY HELPED ME SWEEP THE SIDEWALK.

AH, NICKY, YOU'RE A GOOD BOY! HERE'S TWENTY BUCKS!

AND SO, BECAUSE SHE'S A GIRL, LINDA WAS STIFFED BY GRAMPS. (BUT LATER, NICKY GENEROUSLY GAVE HER HALF THE $20)

men's chores, like taking out the garbage, watching sports on TV, and lifting their feet when their sisters want to vacuum under the chair.

This is not to say that *all* Italian fathers are sexist swine who believe that girls are inferior to boys and should be relegated to a traditional role of female subservience. Occasionally there appears an enlightened Italian dad who believes that girls are as capable as boys of having fulfilling and dynamic careers, successfully carrying on the family business, and bringing pride to the family name. This enlightened attitude, however, occurs only in an Italian father who has no sons. If he has nothing but daughters (or the type of son who sits alone all day in his room watching gladiator movies), the Italian father is likely to find himself to be an ardent advocate of women's rights. Even if his daughters show no interest in the family business, the father knows that there's a good chance that at least one of them will bring into the family a nice, hardworking son-in-law, preferably one who doesn't drive a motorcycle, sport a tattoo, or consider soap-on-a-rope as jewelry.

SURVIVAL TIP #5

Italian Brothers: Never get caught borrowing your sister's records.

SURVIVAL TIP #6

Italian Sisters: Punch your brother only when he's not looking and doesn't know who hit him.

SURVIVAL TIP #7

Italian Brothers: Never throw anything that you cherish at your sister, because you either won't get it back at all or it will be returned torched, splintered, or painfully when you least expect it.

SURVIVAL TIP #8

Italian Sisters: If you must secretly spit in your brother's chocolate milk, do so, but don't tell him about it until either his arm's in a sling, or he's forty-seven years old, or both.

SURVIVAL TIP #9

Italian Brothers: Don't waste your time praying that your sister will be struck blind before she gets a chance to see the damage you did to her car. You'll never have such luck.

SURVIVAL TIP #10

Italian Sisters: Tell your brother that you spilled cranberry juice all over his new white letter sweater person-to-person from Anchorage.

A CAST OF THOUSANDS!

The cast of secondary characters in an Italian family is large and diverse. In non-Italian families, the immediate family consists of the parents, the children, and perhaps the grandparents. Italians, on the other hand, in addition to the parents, children, and grandparents, count aunts and uncles, nephews and nieces, first, second, third, and fourth cousins, great-aunts and great-uncles, anybody once, twice, or three times removed, and just about any paesano just off the boat as members of the immediate family.

It's impossible to describe all the characters in an Italian family; so here are descriptions of some of the more common family members that one might come across:

Cousin Marty: Cousin Marty is Mister Fixit. He's the handiest relative in the family. If something needs to be repaired, he's the man to call. Cousin Marty can do everything from replacing the cellar door to repairing a broken lawnmower. Never mind that sometimes water leaks into the basement and the lawnmower now sounds like a 747, because the only thing Cousin Marty ever expects in exchange for his services is a cup of coffee and a nice chat at the kitchen table.

Marty's favorite expressions are "Sure, instant's fine" and "Nah, just pay me for the parts."

Aunt Josephine: If you look in the encyclopedia under Perpetual Motion, you'll find a picture of Aunt Josephine. She's a bowling alley in stretch slacks. She's incapable of sitting in one position for longer than thirty-seven seconds, and she barrels to the bathroom every

34

twenty minutes, straightening pictures and dusting furniture along the way. She has an unsettling habit of discarding anything that's sitting in one place longer than she is.

"That old thing? I threw it out," is her favorite expression. Magazines, clothing, knickknacks, and small children are not safe in her presence.

Uncle Louie: Uncle Louie is the family entrepreneur. Unfortunately, all of his business projects are collecting dust in his garage and back porch. There, one is likely to find his diesel-powered vibrating mattress, five hundred peel 'n' stick imitation stained-glass kits, and a truckload of green polyester doll hair.

Uncle Louie's favorite expressions are "Guess how much they wanted for it?" and "Guess how much I got it for?"

Uncle Sal: Another businessman, Uncle Sal has a unique filing sys-

The non-Italian bride-to-be meeting a few of her future in-laws.

tem. He stores all of his paperwork and most of his office supplies in the pocket of the shirt he happens to be wearing. Every time Uncle Sal gets out of a chair he stops to search the floor for any item that may have fallen out of his pocket. This action never fails to release the remaining contents of the pocket, and soon the rest of the family is crawling on the floor, retrieving pens, paper clips, and scraps of colored paper.

Uncle Sal is most often heard saying, "What did I drop?" followed by "Nobody move! You might step on something important."

Aunt Mary: Aunt Mary is so old that no one knows for sure how she's related. She's always been there, sitting in the corner of the dining room in her flowered print dress, chewing continually on no one knows what.

Aunt Mary doesn't say much; she just nods her head in agreement to everything that's said. In fact, she says only one thing: "Oh, see that," which she uses in response to every comment. If someone says excitedly that the Balzano house burned to the ground, Aunt Mary will respond sympathetically, "Oh, see that." And if someone else tells her that her cake is delicious, she'll reply proudly, "Oh, see that!"

Uncle Carlo: In every Italian family there's a relative that nobody likes. In this case it's Uncle Carlo. Everybody hates his guts, though nobody can remember the reason they all started hating him; but that's not important. Perhaps he's too rich or too poor. He could be too generous or not generous enough.

The entire family talks about him behind his back. They don't like the way he dresses, the way he combs his hair, the way he talks, his friends, his car, or his after-shave. In his presence they're cordial and nice, but as soon as he's out of earshot they break into gales of laughter and congratulate each other on their constraint and superb performances.

Aunt Carla: Aunt Carla is the female equivalent of Uncle Carlo. She too is universally despised and reviled.

The female members of the family like to pick on Aunt Carla. They criticize her cooking, her hair style, and the shameful way she's raising those kids (who, due to Carla's shortcomings as a mother, are the poor innocent victims of diaper rash, nutritionally deficient breakfasts, ill-fitting shoes, cradle cap, sloppy housekeeping, and Nanna deprivation, i.e., Carla doesn't bring her kids by to see Grandma often enough).

The only good thing that can be said about Carla is that she has a brother-in-law in the wholesale meat business.

Italian child abuse: Saying good-bye to certain relatives.

Cousin Mario: Cousin Mario is a walking Yellow Pages. He knows exactly what you need and how to get it for you. You need a roofer, or a plumber, or an auto mechanic? Mario knows somebody who can handle it for you. You're having a wedding? No problem. Mario himself will handle the catering, and his nephew, Seppi, can get you a deal on the rings. The Martinis will let you use their bowling alley for the reception, and Johnny Piu will handle the photography. Mario's sister-in-law's daughter just got married and she's about the same size as the bride, so hey, he might be able to get a good deal on a slightly used wedding gown. No problem.

Cousin Claudia: Cousin Claudia (aka Claudette) is the family snob. She doesn't mind being considered a snob, just so long as no one considers her an *Italian* snob. Claudia, you see, is trying to hide her Italian heritage. She prefers to pass herself off as French. She has sworn off Italian food; she avoids speaking the language; and she has even named her children Michele, André, and Babs. Claudia looks down her nose at all things Italian. Her phony French façade crumbles, however, whenever she runs into a real French person and is forced to communicate with the only two French phrases she comprehends: "Oui, oui," and "Chevrolet Coupé."

37

Italian philanthropy: Uncles Paulie and Nunzio make generous weekly contributions to the less fortunate.

Aunt Filomina: Aunt Filomina is a conservative old crab who's also a card-carrying religious zealot. As a young girl in the old country, she studied to become a nun, joining the religious order of Little Sisters of the Insolvent, but left the convent after a year because she considered the Sisters' life-style to be too ostentatious.

Filomina still prays in Latin, and believes that women who wear pantsuits are tramps, that lipstick was invented sometime in the eleventh century by Satan himself, and that every Pope since Pius X (1903-14) has been a Communist.

Her favorite expressions are "Hah? What? What did you say?" and "Mark my words, you're going to hell in a handcart!"

SURVIVAL TIP #11

If a strange-looking Italian shows up on your doorstep, greet him like a long-lost relative because he probably is. It will save you time in the long run.

SURVIVAL TIP #12

Be nice to all of your relatives. Where there are wills, there's a way.

"GRANDPA, WHAT BIG POCKETS YOU HAVE!"

Something strange happens to Italians as they approach their golden years. They metamorphose from the conscientious, stern, frugal parents their children knew them as, to become carefree, crazy, and extravagant grandparents. The mom and dad who were inflexible martinets with their own children become sappy little cream puffs with their grandchildren.

Many an Italian daughter remembers trying unsuccessfully to wrangle an extra quarter or two out of Mom to attend the Saturday matinee, only to see that same mother, now a grandmother thirty years later, madly stuffing dollar bills into her grandchildren's pockets; and many a son remembers his old man chasing him down the driveway with a shovel for flushing a banana down the toilet, the same father who now, as a grandparent, staunchly defends his beastly little grandson with a defiant "Don't you lay a finger on that boy. It was your own fault for leaving the car parked on top of a hill."

There are more than a few other similarities among Italian grandparents; and because they are such a diverse lot, the best way to define The Italian Grandparent may be by presenting them individually, in a series of mini-profiles. Then, by studying the similarities that exist in these individual portraits, we might get, if not an accurate composite of The Italian Grandparent, then perhaps an appreciation of their independent natures.

These are real-life profiles of Italian grandparents as related by their own grandchildren.

Tom G.: My grandfather, Pop, had at one time been a successful jeweler and owned three jewelry stores, one downtown and two in the suburbs. He was a fairly wealthy guy, but you'd never know it to look at him. As soon as he retired he started to dress like a bum. He still had lots of money, but he bought his clothes at the Goodwill. He would walk around the neighborhood in these shabby clothes and dig up dandelions to make salads. The neighbors didn't seem to mind. I guess because they were getting their lawns weeded for free.

When we were little, Pop used to try to scare us by telling us that bears and lions lived in the woods behind our house. He once told us that when he was a boy in Sicily there was an earthquake and serpents crawled out of the cracks in the ground and ate all the good little children who ate all their vegetables and drank all their milk. My mom wasn't too crazy about that story.

Greg S.: My mother's mother was Italian and she lived with our family after my grandfather died in 1968.

Granny Dee wore her hair in little braids pinned around her ears and carried a rosary tied to her apron. She wore tennis shoes with holes cut out of them for her bunions, and she used to creep up behind people and scare them to death, swinging her rosary and shrieking like a wild Indian. My little sister still jumps when she hears beads jingling.

Granny had a very annoying way of answering the telephone at our house. No matter what time it rang in the evening, she would answer it by saying, "It's late! Go to bed!" Then she would hang up. It drove my two older sisters insane.

Granny Dee didn't cook much, but when she did, she really knocked herself out. My particular favorites were these cookies she made at Christmastime. They didn't look too appetizing—they were thick and lumpy and you had to pour maple syrup over them—but they were sooooo delicious.

Lucy D.: The fondest memories I have of my grandparents involve my grandmother's kitchen. She always had fresh herbs growing on the windowsill, and the walls were filled with huge copper pots and pans. She made all of her pasta by hand and she used to let us kids roll out the dough and crank it through the pasta maker, which was attached to the edge of the table. We used to collect scraps of the spare dough and make little dough sculptures out of them. She had pierced ears long before it became fashionable. In fact, she'd had them pierced at birth.

Both of my grandparents were very generous. Every Saturday after-

An Italian grandmother's dream turned nightmare.

noon my grandfather, wearing a three-piece suit and smelling of Old Spice, would stop by our house on his way home from the deli. He would give each of us kids a new two-dollar bill and he'd say, "Don't tell your grandmother about this. Let it be our little secret." Then, later that same day we would visit my grandmother and she would pull us aside, slip us each a five-dollar bill, and tell us not to tell "the Old Man," meaning my grandfather. You know, my brothers and I were pretty rich for a bunch of little kids.

Gail S.: My Grandma Lizzie was rather strange. She looked and dressed like a very refined lady who wore hats to drink tea, then she would go down to her cellar and slaughter chickens. She cussed like a sailor and she once said that before the invention of the frozen daiquiri she'd had no reason to live.

She was wild. She once put the malocchio (evil eye) on one of my father's friends, and also on Margaret Truman, but she never told us why. She'd had ten children and she always said that she knew she'd been a good mother because none of her kids had killed each other.

Grandpa Frank, Lizzie's husband, was a retired stonemason and spent his remaining years building patios and sidewalks all around their property. They only had about an acre, so by the time he died at the ripe old age of eighty-seven, he had cemented over just about every available spot of ground. To this day, people stop at his yard, thinking it's some kind of park or something.

Jeff P.: The only grandparent I can remember is my father's mother, who was very short and spoke in a squeaky little voice with a heavy Italian accent. We could never understand what she was saying, so we just agreed with everything she said. She always wore black dresses and black shoes with thick heels. It was the same kind of shoe that nuns used to wear, and I could never figure out where my grandmother bought them, because I never saw shoes like that in any shoe store.

Her house smelled like vinegar, and each room had flowered wallpaper, a different flower for each room. There were red roses in the living room (or the "parlor," as she called it), daisies in the dining room, and some kind of blue weed in my dad's old room.

My grandmother also had a big collection of dolls in a back bedroom. My sister Mary Frances always said that Nanny kept those dolls because late at night, when she was all alone, Nanny would dress up in the doll clothes and parade around in front of the closet mirror.

Well, she was *almost* that small.

Susan L.: Both of my mother's parents were from Italy. Their marriage had been arranged by their families when they were still babies. They got married when they were fourteen or fifteen, and they moved to this country when they were in their twenties.

It was a marriage made in purgatory, if you know what I mean. What I remember most about them is that they argued a lot, in Italian. Very loudly.

My grandfather was almost ninety when he died of a heart attack. My grandmother didn't go to his funeral, so after it was over, I went to visit her to pay my respects. I said to her, "Gee, Nonnie, I'm real sorry and everything," and she said—and I will never forget this—she said, "Lord, I'm glad he's finally gone. Now I can watch what I want to watch on TV."

She really said that, and that's my most vivid memory of her: sitting in a big overstuffed chair, wrapped in an orange afghan, flicking the remote control at the TV.

She died about a year later. I heard she was watching TV at the time.

Tony Z.: My mother's father, Papa Phil, gets mixed reviews. To hear my mom tell about him, you'd think he was this raging tyrant. She says that when she was a girl, he was big and mean and bossy. He worked in a machine parts factory and as soon as he walked through the door at home each night, my mom and her sisters were expected to yank off his heavy work boots. He never allowed my mom or her sisters to wear pants or makeup or fingernail polish, and they weren't allowed to date until they were eighteen.

My mom used to get into terrible arguments with Papa Phil, and one day she got so angry with him that, while he was napping on the couch, she sneaked up on him with a pair of scissors and cut off his mustache. Then she had to stay with a friend for two or three weeks until he cooled off.

As I said, that's her version, and I think she has a tendency to exaggerate, because you should see the man now. First of all, Papa Phil's a shrimp. He's not a bit big. To consider this man big, you'd have to practically be a midget yourself. Secondly, he's the nicest old guy you'd ever want to meet. A real sweetheart. When we grandchildren were little, he always had a smile, a pinch on the cheek, and a half-dollar for each of us. I never heard him yell or argue about anything. So either he underwent a complete transformation from father to grandfather, or my mother really is nuts (something we've suspected for a very long time).

Dan S.: My father's father, Papa "Sto," was a big man who smoked Cuban cigars and spit a lot when he was outside. I don't know what he did indoors. I guess he managed to hold it in.

His wife, Nanna Sto, kept a spotless house and used to say things like, "We might have been poor, but our house was always clean." She was from the Isle of Capri, and to tell you the truth, I once visited Capri and the houses didn't look all that clean to me. I never told her that. If I had, she probably would have smacked me.

Joe N.: Over the years, my grandfather had hundreds of pets. They weren't your usual, run-of-the-mill pets, like dogs or cats, but they were squirrels and chipmunks and baby birds. Every spring he would rescue a baby bird or two that had fallen out of its nest, and if they were injured he would nurse them back to health, sometimes replacing a missing leg with a peg leg made from toothpicks. Everywhere Pop went, the birds would hop along behind.

Pop used to hire this old guy named Greenie to mow the lawn. Greenie was older than Pop, almost ninety, and he couldn't see as far as he could reach. Well, you can pretty much guess the rest of this gruesome tale. One day, while Pop was at the ball game, Greenie ran

Attack of the Killer Grandparents.

over one of the baby birds with the power mower. The bird was named Pete, which is what Pop named all of his animals. We kids found out about it while Pop was still at the game, so we went over to Pop's yard and buried Pete before Pop got home. We were certain that, with Pop's terrible temper, he would pulverize Greenie when he returned that afternoon, so we waited around to catch the show.

Well, we were disappointed. When Pop returned home and Greenie explained what had happened, Pop didn't explode at all. Instead, he paid Greenie for the yard work, sent him home, and disappeared into the tool shed (where we all knew he kept a bottle of Jack Daniel's hidden from my grandmother). A few minutes later he came out and asked us where we had buried Pete. We showed him, and he put a piece of flagstone over the spot to, as he said, "keep the wolves from digging him up." We huddled in silence around that little grave, no one knowing what to say, until my baby sister Gina suddenly recited a Hail Mary. Then we went home.

SURVIVAL TIP #13

When encountering an Italian grandparent, be prepared for anything. Wear a pinch-proof face mask, clothing with oversized pockets, and be ready to diet immediately on disengagement.

"IS YOUR FAMILY ALWAYS LIKE THAT?"

It's unlikely that you'll ever mistake an Italian family for a dull, sensible, "average" family. The Italian family is too unpredictable, loud, spontaneous, and fun to be average.

Compare these average non-Italian families to the Italian families depicted in identical situations.

SURVIVAL TIP #14

In any Italian family in which you find yourself involved, expect drama, noise, turbulence, hysterics, excitement, and fun. Aspirin sometimes helps.

A non-Italian family watching television.

An Italian family watching television.

49

A non-Italian family having dinner at home.

An Italian family having dinner at home.

A non-Italian family playing a trivia game.

An Italian family playing a trivia game.

A non-Italian family on vacation.

An Italian family on vacation.

A non-Italian family not speaking to one another.

An Italian family not speaking to one another.

A non-Italian father spending quality time with his son.

An Italian father spending quality time with his son.

A non-Italian husband consoling his wife.

An Italian husband consoling his wife.

A non-Italian family greeting a returning member at the airport.

An Italian family greeting a returning member at the airport.

Non-Italian parents defending their child.

Italian parents defending their child.

A non-Italian family sharing a humorous story.

An Italian family sharing a humorous story.

A non-Italian family in a crisis.

68

An Italian family in a crisis.

A non-Italian couple discussing a new business venture.

An Italian couple discussing a new business venture.

A non-Italian family at a funeral parlor.

An Italian family at a funeral parlor.

"YOU'RE UGLY
AND
NOBODY LIKES YOU."

How many times have you heard an exasperated Italian say, "Everybody's a critic!"? Plenty of times, I'll bet. That's because in the Italian family, everybody *is* a critic.

Italians love to express their opinions, and those opinions are usually loaded with stinging criticism aimed at any poor soul who might happen to be in the line of fire. They'll criticize everybody and everything, each other as well as themselves. In most Italian families, criticism is called conversation, and everyone from old Uncle Louie who shouts to be heard above the ball game playing on the transistor plugged into his ear, to little cousin Emilio, who still wets his pants every time he hears a beverage being poured, likes to get in on the action. And why not? It's great fun.

The reason there are so many critics in Italian families is that there are so many experts with monstrous egos trying to live together in those same families. Why so many experts and where did they come from?

Well, the requirements for being an expert are not very stringent. Aunt Rosalie read an article in *Seafood Digest* on lobster steamers, so now she's an expert on mercy killing. Uncle Rudy bought a used Buick from a man who grew up on a farm, so Uncle Rudy is now an expert on mulch. Cousin Ramona met a woman at Lexington Market who's brother-in-law is a TV weatherman, so now Ramona is an expert on show business personalities and can tell you who's doing what

to whom in Tinseltown. Such expertise is endless, and with such an abundance of experts in any one family, it makes for some lively conversations around the kitchen table.

With so many experts and so much criticism flying about in a family, it's crucial to protect oneself in the event of an attack. Phrases like "I didn't want to say anything, but . . ." and "I don't want you to take this the wrong way, but . . ." are the first signs of a direct assault. If you find yourself in this unfortunate position, you should first take a deep breath, secure in the knowledge that it really is nothing personal—it happens to everyone—and then confront the attacker head-on. Don't turn your back. It's a sign of weakness and they'll use it to their advantage. Never let an insult go unchallenged. If possible, maneuver yourself into an offensive position. Change the subject if you have to. The important thing to remember is to fight back. It's part of the game and it usually makes for a good show. The rest of the family will appreciate the entertainment value.

75

The following scene between two sisters-in-law actually took place at a crowded family gathering. Only the language has been altered to preserve a PG rating.

Connie notices that her sister-in-law, Stella, who's sitting at the far end of the dinner table, is watching her.

"Stella, what's the matter? You're looking at me funny. Is there something on my dress?"

"No, no, Connie. It's nothing."

Connie begins to clear dishes from the dining room table.

"No, really, Stella. What is it?"

Stella smoothes the napkin in her lap and says, "Well, you know me. I'm not one to say something, but it's your hair."

"What's wrong with it?"

"Nothing. I mean, if that's the way it's supposed to look."

"Like what? I just had it done today."

"At Aileen's? Aileen did that? It doesn't even look like it's been combed."

Connie turns to look at herself in the mirror above the buffet. Uncle Victor, who was about to leave the dinner table to wander into the living room, settles back into his seat. Uncle Ramon peers out over the edge of his newspaper. Grandma rolls her eyes and plops another manicotti onto her plate. This is going to be a good one.

Connie fluffs the hair in back of her head and pulls an errant curl over her forehead. She places her plate on the buffet, turns to Stella, and says, "Stella, you're fat and nobody likes you."

Uncle Victor snorts.

"Oh, shut up, you," says Stella to Victor. "I can't even open my mouth to say two words around here without everybody jumping down my throat! All I was trying to say is that if she paid good money to have her hair look like that, then she was robbed; and for that I'm personally attacked!"

"Don't start with me, Stella. Lay off me and my hair."

"I am not fat!"

"All right, you're *plump* and nobody likes you."

Stella struggles to get out of her chair.

"I know when I've been insulted. Dario!" she shouts to her husband. "Come out of that kitchen and listen to what your sister is saying about me. Take her ass out of the will!"

"Yeah, yeah," mutters Dario from the kitchen.

Stella waddles over to the china closet and by bouncing on one foot, attempts to retrieve her purse from on top; but because dessert

78

hasn't yet been served, she changes her mind and settles down to continue dinner.

Dinner did continue that evening rather uneventfully for an Italian family, with only twenty-eight similar episodes between other family members.

What can we learn from this incident between Connie and Stella? What we can learn can best be summed up by the old axiom: The best defense is a good offense. Or something like that. By leaping to the offense and personally insulting Stella, Connie was able to divert the family's attention from her messy hairdo to Stella's chunky-style hips. Connie has proven that she's an experienced Italian sister-in-law who knows her way around a dinner table.

SURVIVAL TIP #15
Never ask an Italian for his opinion. He might give it to you.

"IF YOU WANT INFORMATION, DIAL 411."

According to recent statistics, for every question posed in an Italian family, the chances are only one in ten that the person asking the question will receive a direct answer. The questioner may get a response, but it won't necessarily be related to the question asked.

This peculiar habit is not exclusive to the Italian family. It's just as difficult to obtain a straight answer in a Jewish family, since it's an ancient Jewish tradition to answer a question with another question. For example, in a Jewish family, "What time is it?" would receive "What, you're in such a big hurry you can't stay and chat for a while?" as a reply.

Italians, on the other hand, avoid answering a question by substituting a lecture for the answer. The lecture can be short and to the point, or lengthy and rambling, and the ideal one is tinged with a spot of guilt. So the same question, "What time is it?" in an Italian family might elicit the response, "Oh, I guess Mister Big Shot can't stay and visit with his family for a few minutes! Nooooo, he's too busy for us. He can't wait to leave!"

Some examples of typical questions and answers in an Italian household:

1. Where's Teresa?
   If you know what's good for you, you'll leave your sister alone!

2. Ma, why are you pacing like that?
   O Dio. Someday you kids will realize what hell you put me through!

3. Any calls for me?
   Oh, yeah, I suppose I'm your personal secretary all of a sudden!

4. So what do you think of my new outfit, huh?
   Go comb your hair before I throw up.

5. What did the doctor say?
   Never mind poor pitiful me. You have more important things to think about, like yourself.

6. Why can't I go to public school like my friends?
   You're giving me a headache, that's why.

7. What are you eating?
   There's never anything to eat in this house!

8. So what did Dad say?
   Curiosity killed the cat, and you're not looking so good yourself.

9. Where's my green sweater?
   Go out dressed like that and you'll kill your mother.

10. Why'd you put so much garlic in the sauce?
    Get a job!

An Italian will sometimes ask a question soliciting someone's opinion on something. Though this rarely occurs, when it does, the question is invariably asked in such a way that only one possible and acceptable response can be elicited.

For example, a non-Italian might ask someone's opinion of his Christmas tree by asking, "What do you think of my tree?" or "How do you like our tree this year?"

In the Italian household, the same question will be phrased: "Isn't this the most beautiful Christmas tree you've ever seen in your entire life?" To a question like that, there's only one possible answer (that is, if you value your life), and that is an enthusiastic *"Yes!"*

Opinion questions are also another way for Italian parents to drive their children crazy with more lectures. An Italian mother complimenting her son in front of others during a dressy occasion might ask, "Isn't he the most handsome son on the face of the earth, if only he had gotten a decent haircut like his father and I begged on bended knees?"

In this case, the mother not only solicits a predetermined compliment, but she also makes known to others, as well as the son, who's surely within earshot, that he'd be perfect if only he would follow exactly his parents' advice.

SURVIVAL TIP #16

When asking a question in an Italian family, expect a lecture, guilt, and/or an insult; anything but a direct answer.

SURVIVAL TIP #17

When an Italian asks for your opinion, always give the expected response, even if you don't agree. You will save yourself the wear and tear of an argument as well as, quite possibly, a smack.

PUMPING PASTA

THE ITALIAN WORKOUT

All Italian families participate in a subtle, low-impact exercise program that starts in the early morning and continues until late at night. This workout is so subtle, in fact, that most Italians are unaware that they're exercising at all.

The Warm-up

All good workouts begin with a warm-up. A few low-resistance, high-repetition warm-up sets pump blood into the muscles, preparing them for the vigorous workout to come. Proper breathing, i.e., exhaling during each movement of resistance, is essential in all exercises, including the warm-up sets.

In The Italian Workout, getting out of bed in the morning constitutes the warm-up, and emitting an involuntary scream while rolling out from under the covers (a practice common to most Italians over the age of thirty) counts as a proper breathing maneuver.

Long-Distance Run

Long-Distance Run

In order to properly perform this exercise, a grandparent or parent is needed to chase another family member around the house, trying to force money upon that person as a gift or as payment for the plastic forks that were bought earlier on sale. This is an excellent workout for the legs and helps build stamina for endurance racing and shopping.

Wrist Curls

Any kind of condiment can be used for this wrist movement, though grated romano or parmesan cheese is recommended. A perfect exercise for strenghtening forearms.

Holy Water Crossovers

An obscure, often neglected exercise, that if done properly, i.e., at least once a week (once a day for the overly devout), helps to build strong chest muscles (unfortunately, on the right side only).

Wrist Curls   Holy Water Crossovers

Italian Aerobics

Italian Aerobics

Aerobics is an excellent means of achieving overall physical fitness, and Italian aerobics offer an added benefit because they can be performed by any Italian, regardless of age, all day long, seven days a week. In fact, some Italians perform these movements in bed at night, while asleep. It's called "talking in one's sleep."

One-Handed Head Smacks

This is an exercise with a double benefit. It's an effective wrist/forearm exercise for the person doing the smacking, and a good neck-strengthening movement for the smackee.

Note: It is suggested that this exercise always be performed with two or more people. Smacking oneself in the head is *not* recommended.

One-Handed Head Smacks

Pasta Pump

Pasta Pump

The idea is to pass heavy plates of pasta and bowls of spaghetti sauce around the dinner table, working the chest muscles and biceps in the process. This exercise should be performed at least three times a day, substituting eggplant, sandwiches, or pancakes when appropriate.

Seated Table-Press

Seated Table-Press

This exercise is performed at the end of each meal by pushing one's chair away from the table. This movement will help to strengthen the chest of a normal-sized person and help build the shoulders of an extremely short person.

THE
ITALIAN FAMILY
SURVIVAL TEST

After you've read the book, take this multiple-choice test to see how you'd fare in an Italian family. The correct answers are at the end of the test.

1. To successfully participate in a conversation in an Italian family, one must have:
   A. Some knowledge of Italian customs and manners.
   B. Basic debating skills.
   C. A good set of lungs.

2. When an Italian mother visits her unmarried daughter, she goes directly to her daughter's bathroom to:
   A. Powder her nose.
   B. Use the facilities.
   C. Check the position of the toilet seat to see if a man has been there.

3. An Italian grandmother believes that using spaghetti sauce from a jar is:
   A. Okay in an emergency.
   B. Fine for snacking only.
   C. The third sign of the Apocalypse.

4. The "slightly chubby" child in an Italian family is:
   A. Usually put on a low-calorie diet.
   B. Urged to get more exercise.
   C. Considered anorexic.

5. The first time an Italian son brings his fiancée, a divorcée with two children, home to meet his family, his mother can usually be found:
   A. In the kitchen, preparing dinner.
   B. In the bathroom, putting out fresh guest towels.
   C. On the roof, ready to jump.

6. The Italian father who frankly and honestly discusses sex education with his children:
   A. Is involved in creative parenting.
   B. Has a healthy relationship with his children, based on mutual trust and respect.
   C. Has had too much to drink and doesn't know what he's doing.

7. The Italian grandmother who remains silent during a family discussion of child-rearing does so because:
   A. She believes that her children know best how to raise their own children.
   B. She believes her own opinions to be too old-fashioned.
   C. She has suffered a stroke and no one has noticed yet.

8. The guest list of a small, intimate Italian wedding, open to the immediate families, includes only:
   A. The parents and siblings of the bride and groom.
   B. The parents, siblings, and grandparents of the bride and groom.
   C. Half the population of New Jersey.

9. The Italian mother who, during a visit to her daughter-in-law's home, has found the house to be messy:
   A. Says nothing, but later sends her daughter-in-law a book of housekeeping hints.
   B. Kindly offers housekeeping suggestions through her son.
   C. Has seen what hell is like.

10. The Italian grandfather who slips his grandchild an extra two dollars every week does so:
    A. To teach the child the value of money.
    B. As an expression of his generosity.
    C. To help keep secret the whereabouts of Grandpa's stash of Jack Daniel's.

11. The Italian grandmother who never cooks, who wears makeup and splashy pantsuits, and who dyes her hair:
    A. Is a truly liberated senior citizen.
    B. Has learned to change with the times.
    C. Is probably French.

12. A "born-again" Italian is one who:
    A. Has reembraced the religion of his youth.
    B. Has visited the land of his roots.
    C. Has eaten seven meatballs in a row and lived to tell about it.

13. The Italian mother who doesn't receive as much as a phone call from her children on her birthday automatically:
    A. Calls them to ask why they haven't called.
    B. Forgets about it and gets on with her life.
    C. Becomes a living martyr.

14. More than anything else, Italian grandmothers hope and pray they find in heaven:
    A. A loving and benevolent God.
    B. Their deceased loved ones.
    C. Bingo.

15. Italian children who are allowed to skip Sunday Mass, live in a messy house, and eat junk food at home:
    A. Have open-minded, free-spirited mothers.
    B. Have mothers with important interests outside the home.
    C. Are orphans.

16. At an Italian funeral, the greatest concern among most of the elderly members of the congregation is:
    A. How the deceased's family is going to cope financially.
    B. How the deceased's family is going to cope emotionally.
    C. What the deceased's family is serving afterward back at the house.

17. Given the choice between living with her Italian mother-in-law or living next door to her Italian mother-in-law, a new bride should:
    A. Choose to live with her mother-in-law.
    B. Choose to live next door to her mother-in-law.
    C. Kill herself.

18. There's always at least one member of an Italian family who collects:
    A. Fine art.
    B. Recordings of Italian operas.
    C. Those little packets of sugar you find in restaurants.

19. To the Italian mother, the new daughter-in-law who avoids family gatherings to spend more time alone with her new husband, is:
    A. An incurable romantic.
    B. A devoted wife.
    C. A nymphomaniac.

20. Many an Italian father falls asleep at night:
    A. Secure in the belief that his children will one day be a source of immense pride.
    B. Aglow in the warmth of a loving and giving family.
    C. In a recliner with a movie in the VCR.

ANSWERS: If you were smart enough to answer C to each of the questions, you're well prepared to survive an Italian family. If you got one or two wrong, reread the book and take the test again. Three or more wrong, and your only hope would be to put yourself up for adoption. Maybe you'll be placed with a nice Danish family.

A BIOGRAPHY OF RICK DETORIE

by Mrs. Giovanna Detorie

When Ricky first wrote his autobiography and showed it to me, I said, "It's real nice. It put me to sleep faster than Uncle Carmine's vacation slides." So he says, "If you don't like it, you write something better." So I did, and here it is. Please excuse any bad spelling or grammar.

My son Ricky—Richard F. Detorie—(or "Rick," as he prefers to be called) was born thirty-some-odd years ago in Baltimore Memorial Hospital. No easy birth, let me tell you, eleven hours I was in labor. But I survived, no thanks to my husband Vince who spent the whole time in the waiting room smoking Kool Filters and talking to a man from Romania.

By the time Ricky started grade school (St. Thomas Aquinas, run by the good School Sisters of Notre Dame—SSND), we were already a regular family, what with the addition of the two girls, Theresa and Sandra Elizabeth. We were also a two-car family with Vince's pick-up and my Impala convertible, painted black and white (the only two-tone Impala in the neighborhood and maybe the world) that we held on to until Kennedy was shot, then we got a '63 Corvair. It was also a convertible.

Ricky did very well in elementary school, getting A's and B's and only one D (penmanship) and got into Loyola High School. It was a fairly expensive school, out in the suburbs and all, but by this time Vince was making good money, having split off from his two brothers to form his own roofing company, "Detour Roofing Company" (clever, huh?).

Ricky did real well at Loyola and liked his Art classes the best. He always had been a good drawer, having won his first drawing contest at four years old when he won a transistor radio from Junket Gelatin for drawing the best TV set. Everyone always said he stayed in the lines better than anybody.

At Loyola Ricky also did a comic strip for the school newspaper. It was a full-page comic soap opera in which all the women had large bosoms and everyone was carrying on with everybody and committing suicide and such. It was pretty racy for a Catholic school paper and some of the parents complained, but it wasn't really all that terrible.

After graduating from Loyola, Ricky went to The Maryland Institute, College of Art, a lovely school with plenty of ample parking. There he majored in graphic design and illustration and minored in painting. He did lots of beautiful paintings, one of which I have hanging in the living room. It's a picture of a girl holding a loaf of bread that looks just like Aunt Rose.

Four years after he entered The Maryland Institute, Ricky graduated with a BFA (cum laude), the first grandchild on the Epifanio side of the family to graduate college. But am I bragging?

Right after college, Ricky moved to Los Angeles where he went to work for a small advertising agency. There he was an art director and creative director and designed all kinds of ads and brochures and stuff and directed photo sessions with beautiful models and movie stars like Farrah Fawcett and Marty Allen and that woman who used to be on Hollywood Squares whose husband died.

While still with the ad agency, Ricky started selling cartoons to magazines like *Saturday Review, Saturday Evening Post,* and *National Lampoon.* Our whole family got a big kick out of those cartoons. One of them had us laughing so hard that Aunt Josie almost wet her pants. Honest to God.

Soon after he left the ad agency Ricky hooked up with Janice and Ross Bagdasarian, a lovely couple who produce The Chipmunks TV show. You know The Chipmunks: Alvin, Simon, and Theodore? Well, Ricky started doing all their artwork. Soon he was designing and illustrating their record albums, story books, games, greeting cards, coloring books, jigsaw puzzles, and even a mustard bottle. He still does Chipmunk work. Most recently he did a cereal box and designed the Chipmunk Meal Packs for Burger King.

Another thing that Ricky does is write cartoon books like *The Official Cat Dictionary* and *No Good Men.* He later did *Totally Tacky Cartoons,* parts I & II and *No Good Lawyers.* One of his most recent was called *Catholics* and it was a personal favorite in our family, seeings how we all went through Catholic schools and the nuns were the same fifty years ago as they are today, believe you me.

As for personal information, Ricky is healthy and single. Come to think of it, all three of my children are still single; but that doesn't bother me, seeings how most kids nowadays get married and divorced like they're changing clothes. I don't believe in getting involved in my kids' affairs. For example, if Ricky had wanted to marry that ditsy waitress from Annapolis, I wouldn't have said two words. Really.

Well, that's about it. Someone once asked me if I thought I raised my kids right. The way I figure it, they got lots of love and vitamins when they were little and they're still speaking to me now, so that must mean something.

Sincerely,
Giovanna Detorie